Oxford Read and Discover

In the Sky

T0344563

Kamini Khanduri

Contents

OXFORD
UNIVERSITY PRESS

OXFORD
UNIVERSITY PRESS

Great Clarendon Street, Oxford, OX2 6DP, United Kingdom

Oxford University Press is a department of the University
of Oxford. It furthers the University's objective of excellence in
research, scholarship, and education by publishing worldwide.
Oxford is a registered trade mark of Oxford University Press
in the UK and in certain other countries

First published in 2012

2019

16

No unauthorized photocopying

ISBN: 978 0 19 464630 7

An Audio Pack containing this book and an Audio download is
also available, ISBN 978 0 19 402141 8

This book is also available as an e-Book,
ISBN 978 0 19 410842 3.

An accompanying Activity Book is also available,
ISBN 978 0 19 464651 2

Printed in China

This book is printed on paper from certified and
well-managed sources.

ACKNOWLEDGEMENTS

Illustrations by: Kelly Kennedy pp.5, 8, 10, 13, 15, 23; Alan Rowe
pp.20, 21, 22, 24, 25, 26, 27, 30, 31.

*The Publishers would also like to thank the following for their kind
permission to reproduce photographs and other copyright material*:
Alamy pp.6 (crescent moon/Manfred Mothes/F1online digitale
Bildagentur GmbH), 12 (Dennis Hallinan); Corbis pp.7 (stars/
Roger Ressmeyer, planet/Kennan Ward), 11 (Rio by night/
Danny Lehman), 13 (© NASA – Hubble Heritage – digital/
Science Faction), 16; Getty Images p.11 (Rio by day/IIC/Axiom);
Oxford University Press pp.3 (day sky/night sky), 4, 6 (full
moon), 15 (© NASA/Corbis), 17 (footprint); Science Photo
Library pp.5 (Cordelia Molloy), 8 (NASA/LMSAL), 9 (Detlev Van
Ravenswaay), 14 (Claus Lunau), 17 (astronaut/NASA), 18 (space
shuttle and ISS/astronauts/NASA), 19 (NASA).

 # Introduction

Go outside and look up. What can you see? You can see the sky. The sky is above you.

day

night

Look at the sky. Is it day or night? What can you see in the sky?

 Now read and discover more about the sky!

1 The Sky

In the Day

Look at the sky in the day. What
color is it? Can you see clouds?
When it's sunny, the sky is blue.
Clouds are white or gray.
Sometimes you can see birds
and planes. They fly in the sky.

A Rainbow

Sometimes when it's sunny and rainy, you can see a rainbow in the sky. How many colors can you see?

A spacecraft goes up into the sky. Then it goes into space. Space is dark and very big.

space

sky

→ Go to page 20 for activities.

At Night

At night the sky is dark. You can see the moon. The moon is a big ball of rock.

Sometimes you see a round moon. This is called a full moon. Sometimes you see different shapes. A thin moon is called a crescent moon.

A Full Moon

A Crescent Moon

You can see stars at night, too. Stars are big, hot balls of fire. They look very little because they are far out in space. Sometimes you can see planets, too.

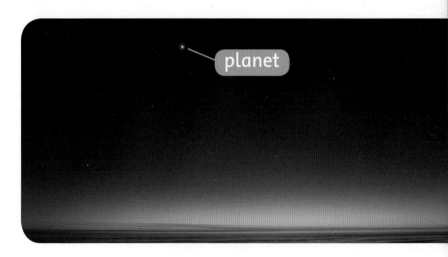

planet

→ Go to page 21 for activities.

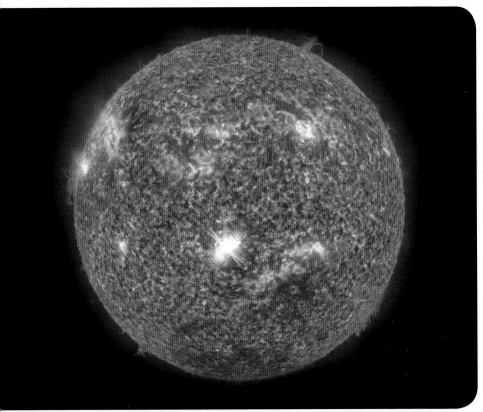

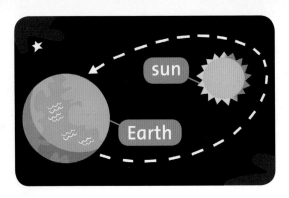

Do you know the sun is a star? It's our star. We live on a planet called Earth. Earth goes around the sun.

The sun shines in the sky. It gives our planet light. Don't look at the sun. It isn't good for your eyes.

The sun is very, very hot. It makes our planet warm so we can live here.

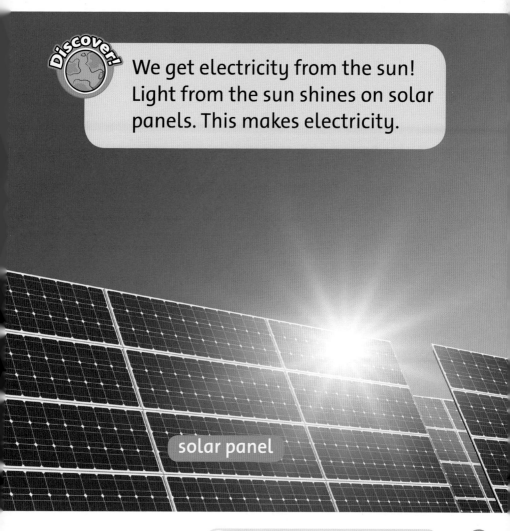

Discover!

We get electricity from the sun! Light from the sun shines on solar panels. This makes electricity.

solar panel

Go to page 22 for activities.

Day and Night

Sometimes it's day and sometimes it's night. That's because Earth turns.

When your place on Earth turns toward the sun, you see light from the sun. This is day.

When your place turns away from the sun, you don't see light from the sun. This is night. Then Earth turns and it's day again.

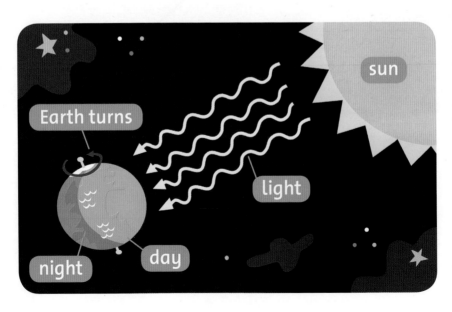

sun

Earth turns

light

night

day

In the Day

At Night

At night it's dark. It's dark in parks and gardens. It's dark in homes, too. People make light with electricity or candles. Is it dark when you go to bed?

→ Go to page 23 for activities.

5 Stars

Stars can look red, orange, yellow, blue, or white. The sun is a yellow star. You can see patterns of stars in the sky. The patterns are called constellations.

With a telescope, you can see more stars. The Hubble Space Telescope is a very big telescope out in space. It takes photos of stars.

The Hubble Space Telescope

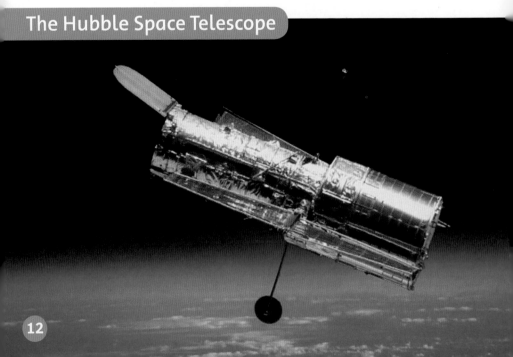

A Galaxy

A galaxy is lots of stars. There are many millions of stars in one galaxy. Our galaxy is called The Milky Way.

Discover!

Old stars don't live for ever, but there are new stars, too!

→ Go to page 24 for activities.

6 Planets

A planet goes around a star.
Eight planets go around the sun.
The sun and its planets are
called the solar system.

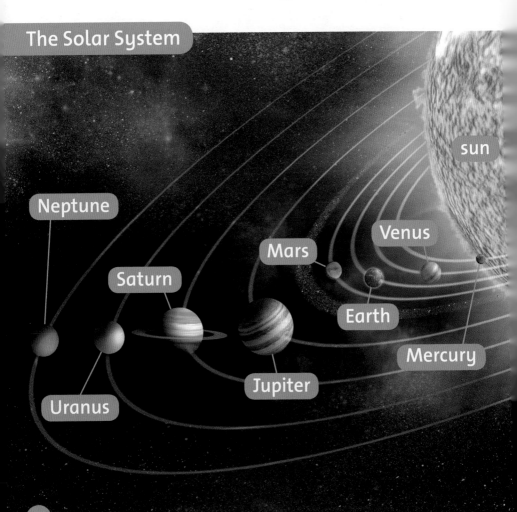

The Solar System

sun

Neptune

Venus

Mars

Saturn

Earth

Jupiter

Mercury

Uranus

The planets are all different.
Jupiter is big and Mercury is little.
Venus is hot and Neptune is cold.
Saturn has lots of rings.

Earth

the moon

Many planets have moons. A moon goes around a planet. Earth has one moon. We call it the moon. Some planets have lots of moons.

Discover!

The planet Saturn has about 60 moons!

→ Go to page 25 for activities.

7 On the Moon

crater

On the moon there's dust and rock. There are tall mountains, and big holes called craters. There's black space all around, and no blue sky. There's no weather because there's no sky. It's hot in the day and it's cold at night.

tank

An Astronaut

Astronauts can go to the moon.
This astronaut is on the moon.
How amazing! He has a space
suit and he breathes air
from a tank.

Footprints are on the moon
for a million years! There's
no wind to blow them away.

Go to page 26 for activities.

8 Into Space

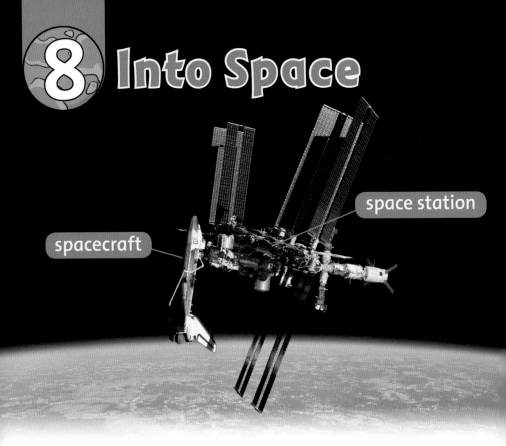

spacecraft

space station

Astronauts go into space. They go in a spacecraft.

Astronauts

Astronauts can live in space. They live in a space station. They look at Earth and learn about it.

Spacecraft with no people in them go into space, too. Some spacecraft take photos of Earth and space. Some spacecraft go to other planets so we can learn about them.

Maybe one day you can go into space, too!

A Spacecraft

Go to page 27 for activities.

1 The Sky

← Read pages 4–5.

1 Write the words.

sky   spacecraft   cloud
plane   ~~bird~~   rainbow

1 ___bird___

2 _____

3 _____

4 _____

5 _____

6 _____

2 Complete the sentences.

big   ~~sky~~   rainbow   space

1 A spacecraft goes up into the ___sky___ .
   Then it goes into _____ .

2 Space is dark and very _____ .

3 Sometimes when it's sunny and rainy,
   you can see a _____ .

② At Night

← Read pages 6–7.

1 Write *true* or *false*.

1 In the day the sky is dark.   *false*

2 At night you can see the moon.   _____

3 The moon is a big ball of fire.   _____

4 A round moon is called a full moon.   _____

5 A fat moon is called a crescent moon.   _____

2 Write the words. Then match.

1 o n o m

___*moon*___

2 r a s s t

_____

3 o r k c

_____

4 r e i f

_____

← Read pages 8–9.

1 Circle the correct words.

1 The sun is a **planet** / **star.**

2 We live on a planet called **Earth** / **eyes.**

3 Earth goes around the **moon** / **sun.**

4 The sun is very, very **hot** / **cold.**

5 **Look** / **Don't look** at the sun.

2 Complete the puzzle.

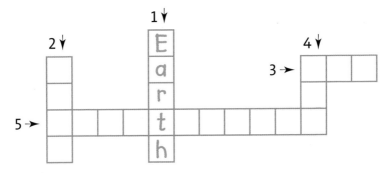

4 Day and Night

← Read pages 10–11.

1 Write the words.

| sun | day | light |
| Earth | night |

1 _____ 2 _____ 3 _____

4 _____ 5 _____

2 Write *true* or *false*.

1 Earth turns. _____

2 In the day, you don't see light from the sun. _____

3 At night you see the sun. _____

4 People make light with electricity. _____

5 Stars

← Read pages 12–13.

1 Find and write the words.

g	a	p	h	o	t	o	x	y
t	e	l	i	l	y	s	o	t
c	o	p	g	a	l	a	x	y
s	t	a	r	s	s	t	r	n
p	a	t	t	e	r	n	l	t
t	e	l	e	s	c	o	p	e

1 _stars_

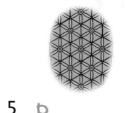

2 t_____

3 g_____   4 p_____   5 p_____

2 Circle the correct words.

1 The sun is a **red** / **yellow** star.

2 Patterns of stars are called **constellations** / **photos**.

3 With a **pattern** / **telescope**, you can see more stars.

4 The Milky Way is our **galaxy** / **sun**.

6 Planets

← Read pages 14–15.

1 Write the words.

Venus   Mercury
Neptune   Earth   Saturn
Jupiter   Mars   Uranus

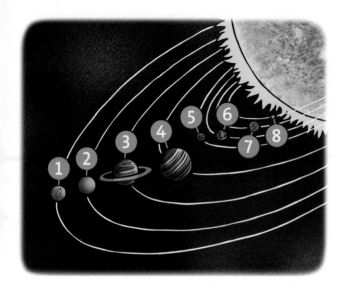

1 _____

2 _____

3 _____

4 _____

5 _____

6 _____

7 _____

8 _____

2 Complete the sentences.

one   solar   Saturn   Eight

1 _____ planets go around our sun.

2 The sun and its planets are called the _____ system.

3 _____ has lots of rings.

4 Earth has _____ moon.

25

7 On the Moon

← Read pages 16–17.

1 Write the words.

hole	breathe	rock
dust	wind	mountains

1 _____   2 _____   3 _____

4 _____   5 _____   6 _____

2 Match. Then write the sentences.

Astronauts can go to   space suits.
Astronauts have   from a tank.
Astronauts breathe air   the moon.

1 _Astronauts can go to the moon._

2 _____

3 _____

8 Into Space

← Read pages 18–19.

1 Complete the sentences.

photos   planets
station   space

1 Astronauts go into _____ in a spacecraft.

2 Some spacecraft take _____ .

3 Some spacecraft go to other _____ .

4 Astronauts live in a space _____ .

2 Complete the puzzle.

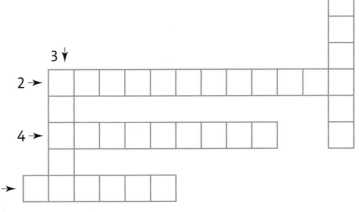

Project: The Sky Where I Live

1 Look at the sky in the day. Complete the chart.

	Day 1	Day 2
What color is the sky?		
Are there clouds?		
Are there birds?		
Can you see the sun?		
What other things can you see?		

2 Look at the sky at night. Complete the chart.

	Night 1	Night 2
What color is the sky?		
Can you see any lights?		
Is there a moon?		
Are there stars?		
What other things can you see?		

3 Look at your charts. Find or draw pictures and write sentences about the sky.

In the day the sky is _____

There are _____

_____

_____

At night _____

_____

_____

_____

Picture Dictionary

above

air

around

bed

blow

breathe

candle

dark

dust

Earth

electricity

far

fire

hole

light

million

mountains   pattern   photo   plane

  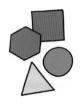

planet   ring   rock   shapes

sky   space   spacecraft   space suit

sun   telescope   up   warm

Oxford Read and Discover

Series Editor: Hazel Geatches • CLIL Adviser: John Clegg

Oxford Read and Discover graded readers are at six levels, for students from age 6 and older. They cover many topics within three subject areas, and support English across the curriculum, or Content and Language Integrated Learning (CLIL).

Available for each reader:
• Audio Pack
• Activity Book

Available for selected readers:
• e-Books

Teaching notes & CLIL guidance: **www.oup.com/elt/teacher/readanddiscover**

Subject Area / Level	The World of Science & Technology	The Natural World	The World of Arts & Social Studies
1 300 headwords	• Eyes • Fruit • Trees • Wheels	• At the Beach • In the Sky • Wild Cats • Young Animals	• Art • Schools
2 450 headwords	• Electricity • Plastic • Sunny and Rainy • Your Body	• Camouflage • Earth • Farms • In the Mountains	• Cities • Jobs
3 600 headwords	• How We Make Products • Sound and Music • Super Structures • Your Five Senses	• Amazing Minibeasts • Animals in the Air • Life in Rainforests • Wonderful Water	• Festivals Around the World • Free Time Around the World
4 750 headwords	• All About Plants • How to Stay Healthy • Machines Then and Now • Why We Recycle	• All About Desert Life • All About Ocean Life • Animals at Night • Incredible Earth	• Animals in Art • Wonders of the Past
5 900 headwords	• Materials to Products • Medicine Then and Now • Transportation Then and Now • Wild Weather	• All About Islands • Animal Life Cycles • Exploring Our World • Great Migrations	• Homes Around the World • Our World in Art
6 1,050 headwords	• Cells and Microbes • Clothes Then and Now • Incredible Energy • Your Amazing Body	• All About Space • Caring for Our Planet • Earth Then and Now • Wonderful Ecosystems	• Food Around the World • Helping Around the World